CHART HITS NOW!

BURN

...PLUS 11 MORE TOP HITS

Published by
Wise Publications
14-15 Berners Street, London W1T 3LJ, UK.

Exclusive Distributors:

Music Sales Limited
Distribution Centre, Newmarket Road,
Bury St Edmunds, Suffolk IP33 3YB, UK.

Music Sales Pty Limited
Units 3-4, 17 Willfox Street,
Condell Park, NSW 2200, Australia.

Order No. AM1008095
ISBN: 978-1-78305-405-3
This book © Copyright 2013 Wise Publications,
a division of Music Sales Limited.

Edited by Jenni Norey.
Cover design by Tim Field.

Printed in the EU.

CHART HITS NOW!

PIANO • VOCAL • GUITAR

BURN

...PLUS 11 MORE TOP HITS

WISE PUBLICATIONS
part of The Music Sales Group
London / New York / Paris / Sydney / Copenhagen / Berlin / Madrid / Hong Kong / Tokyo

Atlas

Words & Music by Guy Berryman, Jonathan Buckland,
William Champion & Christopher Martin

1. Some saw_____ the sun.

Some saw_____ the smoke.
Some far_____ a - way.

Caught in_____ the fire. Say "oh,__
Show me_____ the way, Lord, 'cause I'm,__

we're a - bout_____ to ex -
I'm a - bout_____ to ex -

- plode." }
- plode. }
'Car - ry your world._____

I'll car - ry your world._____

8

Car-ry your world.

I'll car-ry your world.

(Car-ry your world.) Car-ry your world

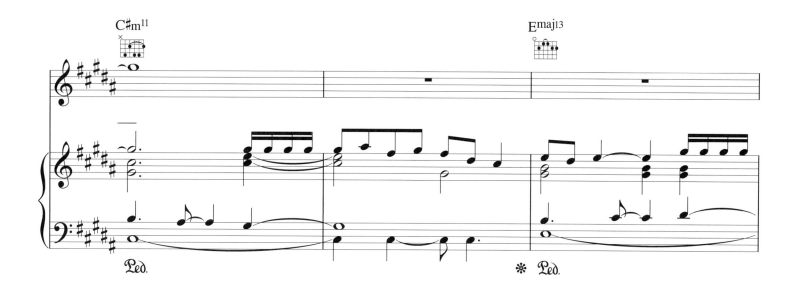

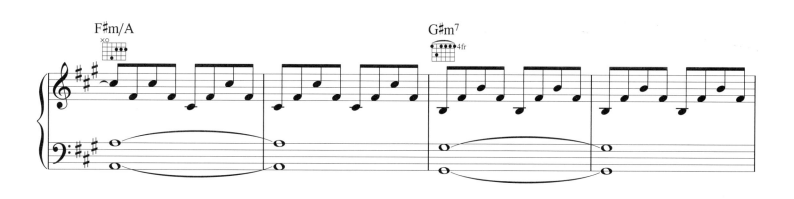
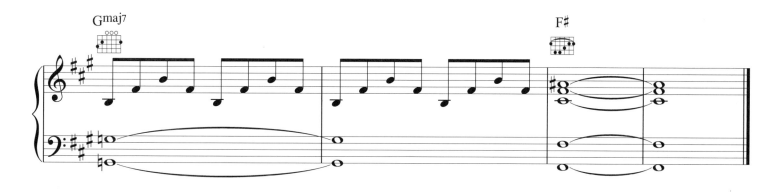

Applause

Words & Music by Stefani Germanotta, Paul Blair,
Nick Monson, Dino Zisis & Martin Bresso

1. I stand here wait - ing___ for you to bang___ the gong.___
2. I've o - ver - heard___ your theo - ry "nos - tal - gia's for geeks."

To crash the cri-tic say-ing "Is it right or is it wrong?"___
I guess sir, if you say___ so, some of us just like to read.___

N.C.

If on-ly fame had an___ I. V. ba-by, could I bear___
One sec-ond I'm a Koons then sud-den-ly the Koons is me.___

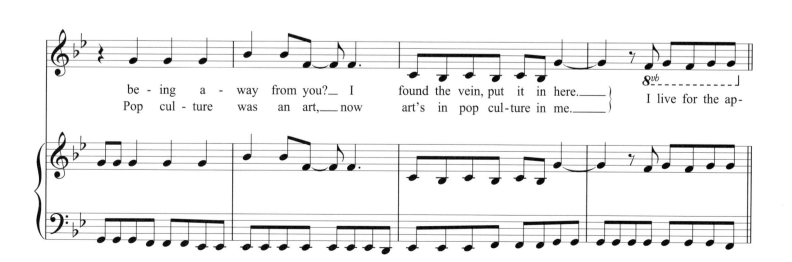

be-ing a-way from you?___ I found the vein, put it in here.___
Pop cul-ture was an art,___ now art's in pop cul-ture in me.___

I live for the ap-

Put your hands up, make 'em touch.___ (Make it real loud.) (A P P L A U_

___ S E.)___
(Make it real loud.)
Put your hands up, make 'em touch,___ touch.___ (A P P L A U_

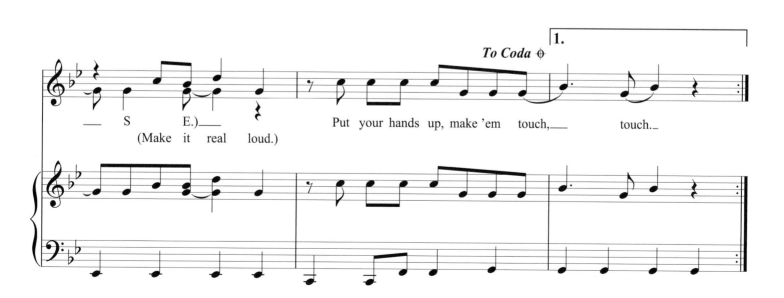

To Coda ✛

1.

___ S E.)___
(Make it real loud.)
Put your hands up, make 'em touch,___ touch._

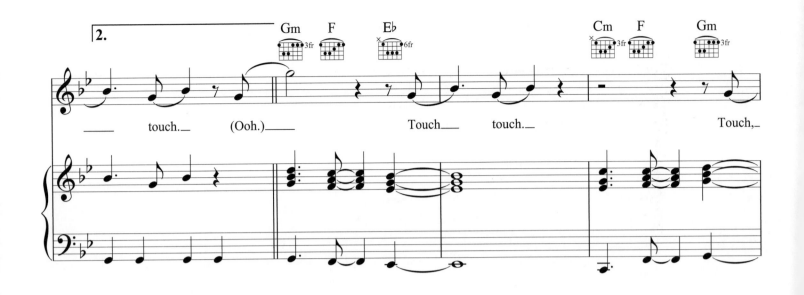

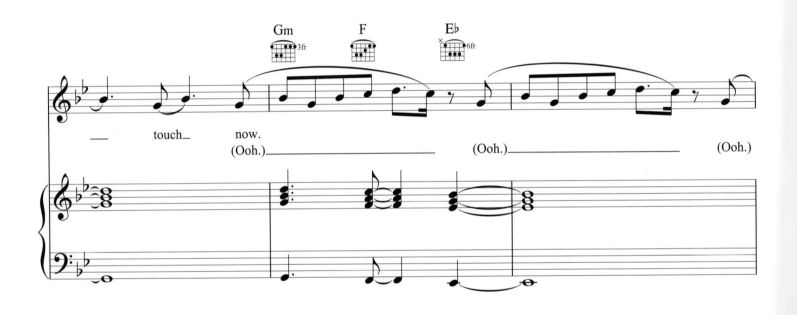

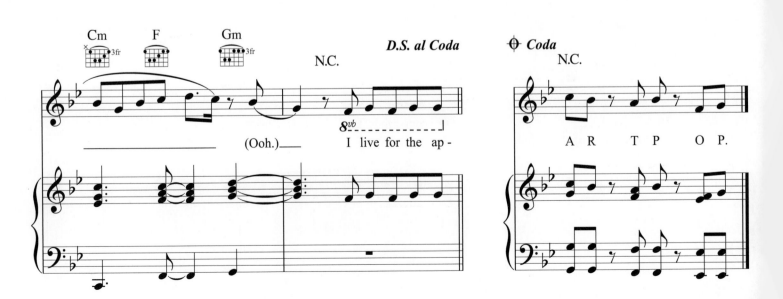

16

Best Song Ever

Words & Music by Wayne Hector, John Ryan,
Julian Bunetta & Edward Drewett

1. May - be it's the way she walked straight in - to my heart and stole
2. Said her name was Geor - gia Rose and her dad - dy was a den -

20

Burn

Words & Music by Greg Kurstin, Ryan Tedder,
Brent Kutzle, Noel Zancanella & Elena Goulding

1. We,—

(2.) leave,   no,   we don't have to wor-ry 'bout noth - ing,—   'cause we got the fire—
                     we just wan-na be right— now.—   And what we see—

play it loud, _____ giv-ing love _____ to the world. ____ We're gon-na let it

burn, burn, ___ burn, ___ burn, ___ burn, burn.

We can light it up, up, ___ up so they can't put it out, out, ___ out. We can light it

up, up, ___ up so they can't put it out, out, ___ out. We can light it

Blurred Lines

Words & Music by Pharrell Williams, Robin Thicke
& Clifford Harris

If you can't hear what I'm try'n' to say, if you can't read from the same page, may-be I'm go-ing deaf, may-be I'm go-ing blind, may-be I'm out of my mind.

O K, now he was close, tried to do-mes-ti-cate you.

But you're an a-ni-mal, ba-by it's in your na-ture. Just let me li-be-rate you.

You don't need no pa-pers. That man is not your ma-ker. And that's why I'm gon' take a

good girl._____ I know you want it. I know you want it.

I know you want it. You're a good girl._____

32

Can't let it get past me. You're far from plas-tic. Talk a-bout get-tin' blast-ed. I hate these

blurred lines. I know you want it. I know you want it.

I know you want it. But you're a good girl. The way you grab me,

To Coda ⊕

must wan-na get nas-ty. Go a-head, get at me.

What do they make dreams for? When you got them jeans on, what do we need steam for?

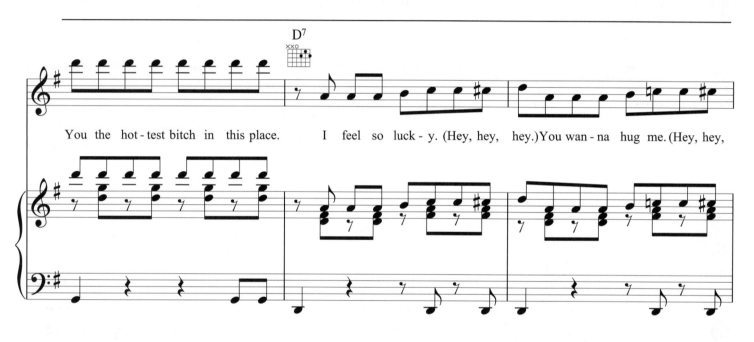

You the hot-test bitch in this place. I feel so luck-y. (Hey, hey, hey.) You wan-na hug me. (Hey, hey,

hey.) What rhymes with hug me? (Hey, hey, hey.)
Hey...

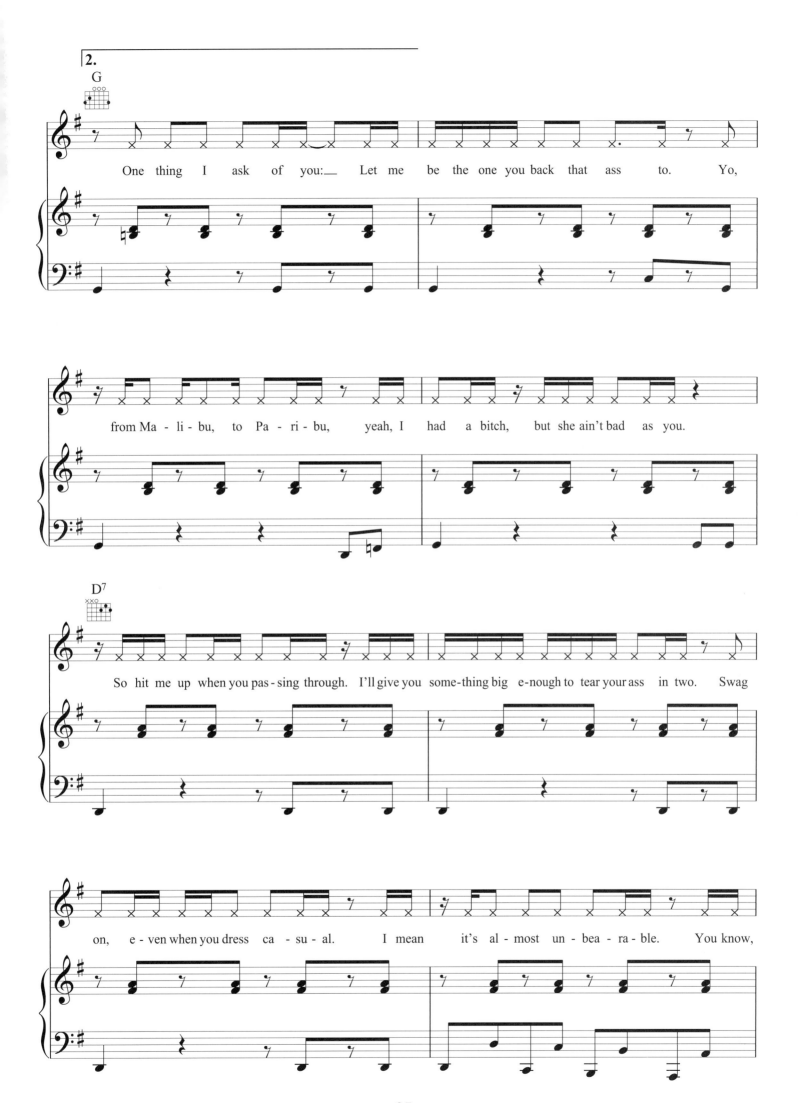

G

hon-ey you're not there when I'm with my fore-sight, bitch, you pay me by.

Noth-ing like your last guy, he too square for you. He don't smack that ass and pull your hair like that. So I

D7

just watch and wait for you to sa-lute. But you did-n't pick.

Not man-y wom-en can re-fuse this pimp-in'. I'm a nice guy, but you get it if you get with me.

Flatline

Words & Music by Keisha Buchanan, Mutya Buena,
Siobhan Donaghy & Devon Hynes

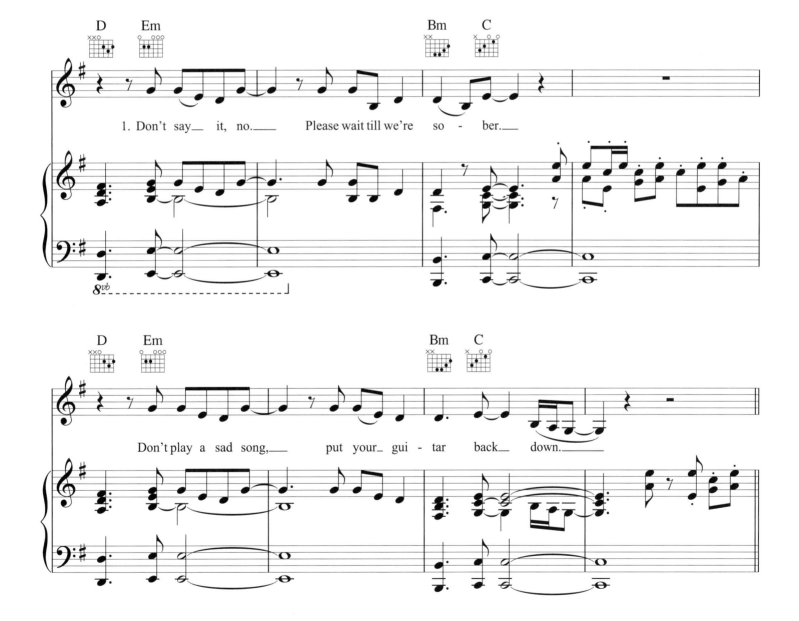

41

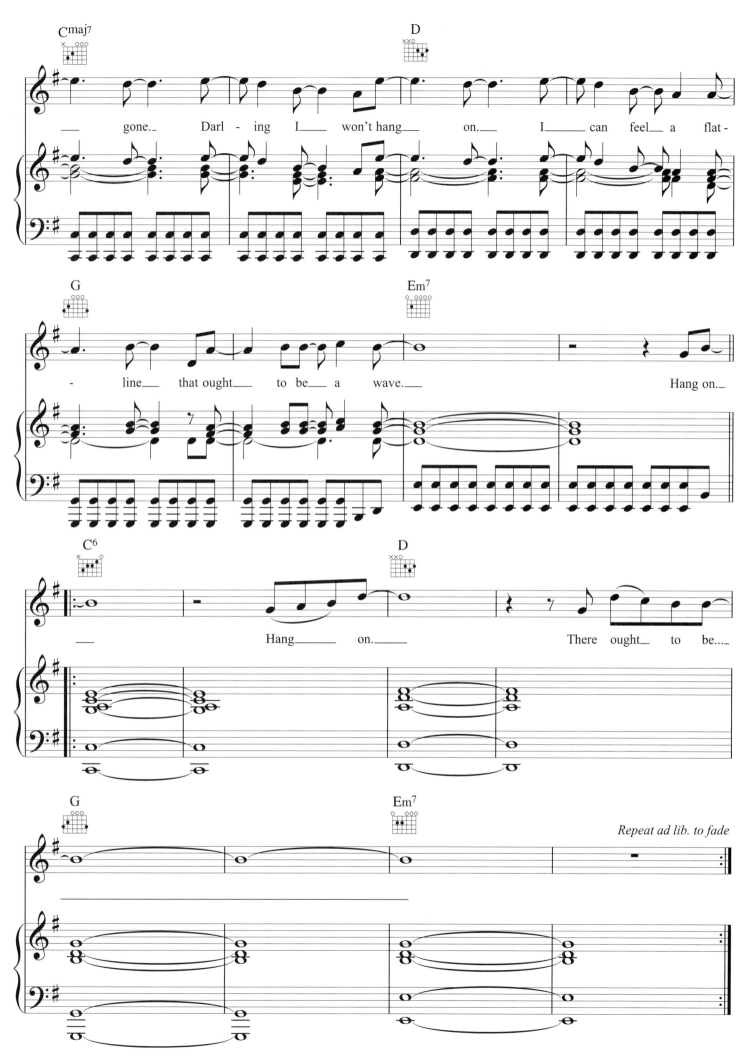

Love Like This

Words & Music by Mark Prendergast, Vincent May
& Stephen Garrigan

1. Run-ning through the heat, heart beat, you shine like
2. Slip-ping into the night love, it grows dark but you don't mind.

47

48

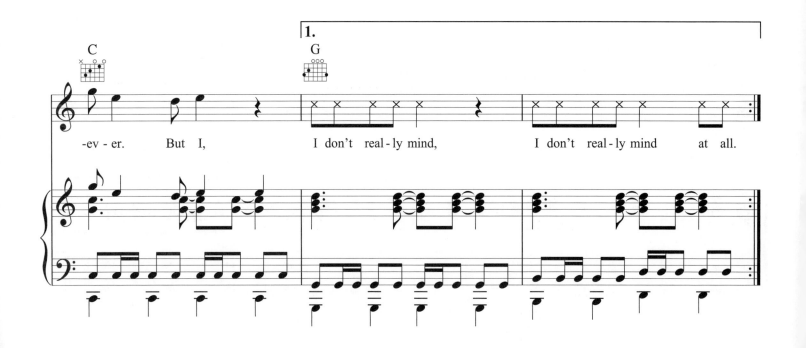

-ev - er.   But I,   I don't real - ly mind,   I don't real - ly mind   at all.

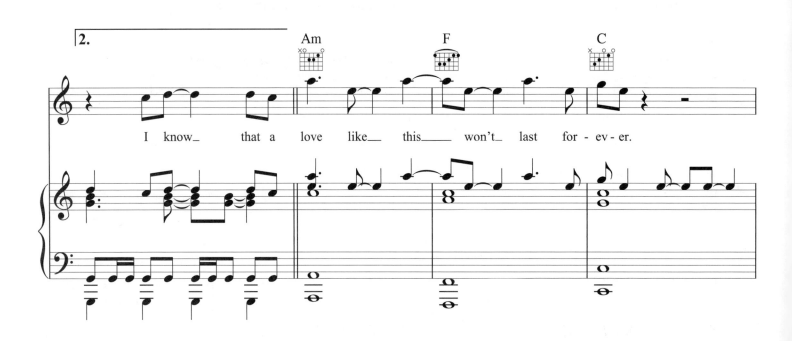

I know_   that a   love   like_   this_   won't_   last   for - ev - er.

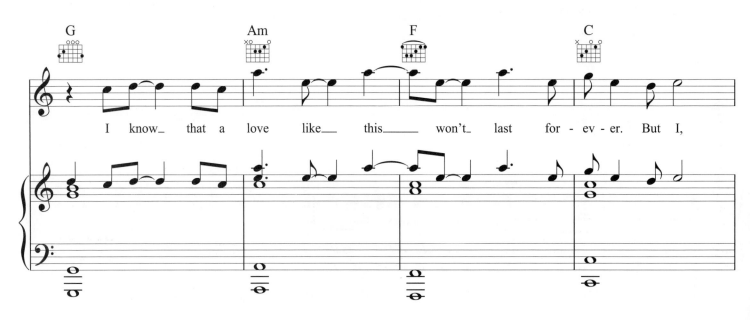

I know_   that a   love   like_   this_   won't_   last   for - ev - er.   But I,

Roar

Words & Music by Lukasz Gottwald, Bonnie McKee,
Katy Perry, Martin Max & Henry Russell Walter

Lou - der, lou - der than the li - on. 'Cause I am a cham - pion and you're gon - na hear me roar. Oh, oh, oh, oh, oh.

Oh, oh, oh, oh, oh, oh. Oh, oh, oh, oh, oh, oh.

1.
You're gon - na hear me roar.

2, 3.
Oh, oh, oh, oh, oh.

Perc.

56

She

Words & Music by Steven Brown & Laura Mvula

1.% She walked to-wards you with her head down low,
2. There she waits look-ing for a sa - viour,

she won-dered if there's a way out of the blue.
some - one to save her from her dy - ing self.

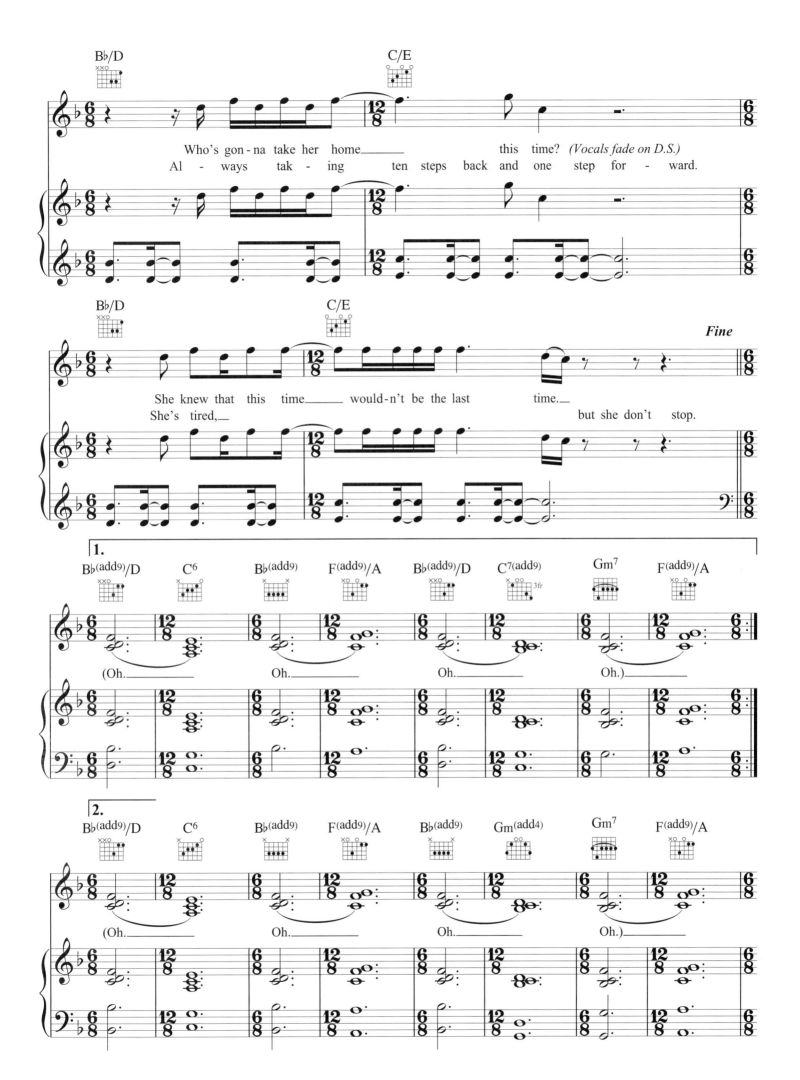

Summertime Sadness

Words & Music by Richard Nowels & Elizabeth Grant

Kiss me hard be - fore you go,___ sum - mer - time sad - ness.___

I just wan - ted you to know___ that, ba - by, you the best.___ 1. I got my

66

Got that sum-mer-time, sum-mer-time sad-ness. Oh, oh,_____ oh._____

Wake Me Up

Words & Music by Aloe Blacc, Tim Bergling
& Michael Einziger

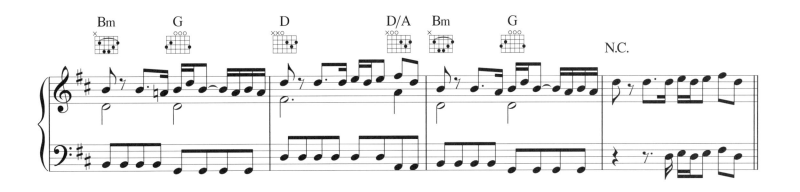

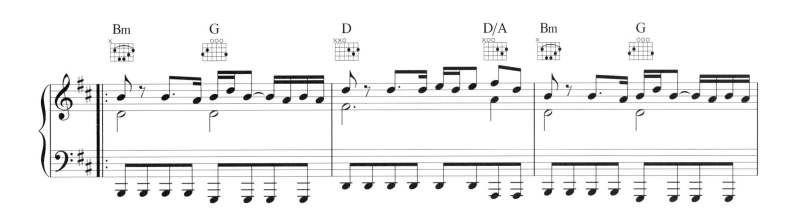

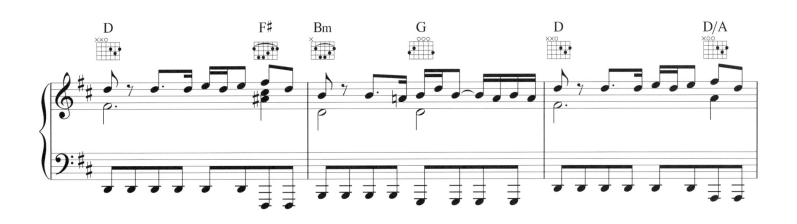

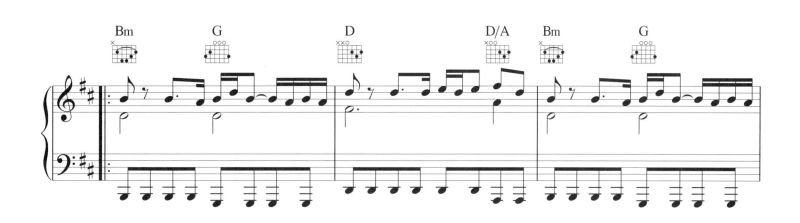

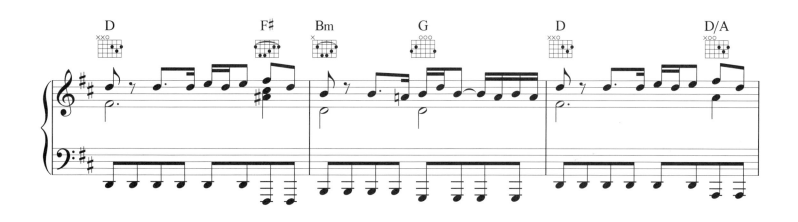

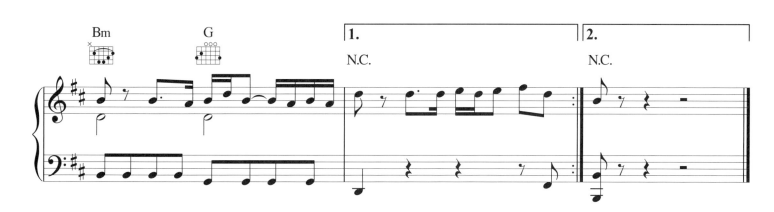

We Can't Stop

Words & Music by Ricky Walters, Douglas Davis, Miley Cyrus,
Michael Williams, Theron Thomas, Timothy Thomas & Pierre Slaughter

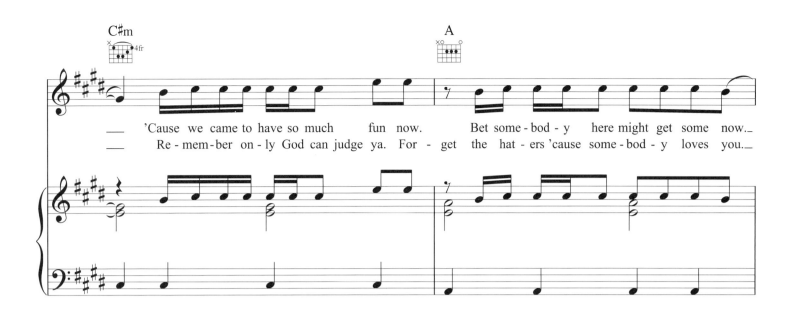

'Cause we came to have so much fun now. Bet some-bod - y here might get some now._
Re - mem - ber on - ly God can judge ya. For - get the hat - ers 'cause some - bod - y loves you._

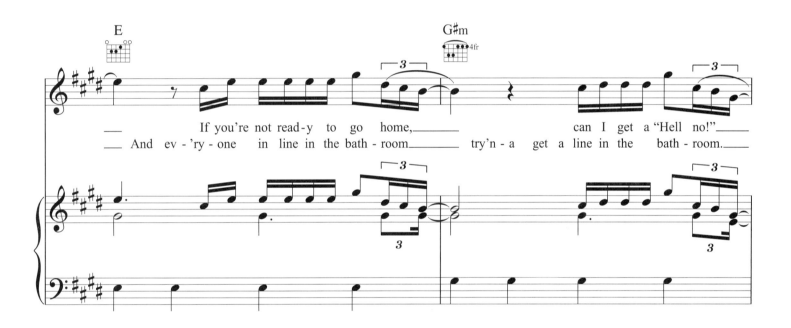

If you're not read-y to go home,_ can I get a "Hell no!"_
And ev - 'ry - one in line in the bath - room_ try'n - a get a line in the bath - room._

'Cause we're gon - na go all night till we see the sun - light. Al - right._ } So
We all so turned up here. Get - ting turned up, yeah, yeah.

123456789